The Tree Frog

Adapted from an idea by Syunichi Ueno
Illustrated by Takayuki Sakaguchi
Consultant for English language version: Ralph Whitlock

Wayland

Where is the frog?

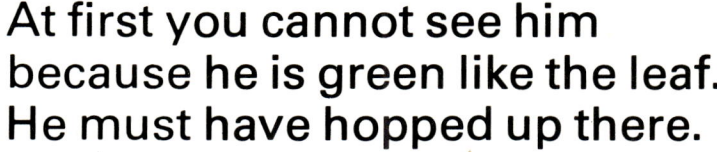

At first you cannot see him
because he is green like the leaf.
He must have hopped up there.

He is a tree frog, but he lives in bushes and grass as well as in trees. He is getting ready to jump again.

There he goes!

If you touch him his skin is cold
and wet. If his skin gets dry he
cannot breathe. So he must keep it
wet all the time.

Now he is sitting on a rock.

Look! He has changed colour. He is the same colour as the rock. Now birds and snakes looking for a dinner will not be able to see him.

Tree frogs have little suckers at the tips of their fingers. They can stick to anything. So the frog can climb without sliding down. He can climb fast, too.

Now he is at the top of the pole. He has caught an insect. Frogs eat live insects. But sometimes they catch a falling leaf and eat it, thinking it is an insect.

Frogs croak before it rains. Also, the males croak when they want to attract females.

This frog is swelling like a balloon. He is getting ready to sing!

This small brown frog has air bags in his cheeks. He is called a Leopard Frog, because of his spots.

He fills up his throat bags with air. It makes a noise when he lets it out again. He thinks it is singing, but we would call it croaking.

Now we have two frogs.

A female has joined the male. They are jumping together.

Because of its long back legs, a frog can jump ten or twenty times the length of its body.

This is the female frog. She is going to lay her eggs on the leaves of the water plants. See how she swims with her eyes half out of the water. It looks as though she is wearing goggles.

Now the frog's eggs have hatched.

The young frogs are called tadpoles. They are little black blobs with tails. They are swimming round and round in the pond. The frog laid only 20 or 30 eggs, so some of these tadpoles must belong to another frog.

The eggs are lumps of white jelly with black spots in the middle.

First the black spots grow into tiny tadpoles. After 20 days the tadpole can swim away.

Then, after 50 more days, the hind legs begin to grow. At the same time the tail is becoming smaller.

After two more weeks the tadpole grows its front feet, first the right one, then the left one.

At last the tadpole has become a frog. His tail has gone. And now he can come out of the water and walk on the land.

But he is still small. It will take him
three years to become full-grown.

These are some members of the
frog and toad family:

Leopard frog

Tree frog

Bullfrog

Toad

HOW TO LOOK AFTER TADPOLES

Put stones in the bottom of a glass tank. Add one big rock, and fasten some water grass under it. Pour in water till the tank is more than half full. Do not quite cover the big rock with water.

Put the tadpoles or eggs into the water. Feed them with bread crumbs, egg yolk, spinach, rice and little pieces of dried fish. Give them only a little at a time. If the tadpoles have more than they can eat, the food will stay in the water and make it dirty.

When the tadpoles have grown arms and legs and their tails have become short, they will start to climb on the big rock.

When they have become frogs it is best to take them to a pond or river and let them go. They will not be happy in the tank any longer.

29

Only three kinds of frog live in Britain, and two of those are very rare. But common frogs come in many different colours — green, yellow, brown, red, and spotted.

In autumn, frogs find a hole in a bank of a stream or bury themselves in mud at the bottom of a pond. There they go to sleep for the winter. Early in spring they wake up to lay their eggs.

The eggs are called spawn. They are stuck together in a mass like jelly.

The spawn of toads is different. It is linked together like beads on a string. A toad is very like a frog but it has a dry, knobbly skin. It lives on the land most of the time, but it goes to the water to lay its eggs. There is a picture of a toad on page 27.

ISBN 0 85340 682 0

Copyright © 1977, 1979 by Froebel-Kan Ltd., Tokyo
First published in English in 1979 by
Wayland Publishers Limited
49 Lansdowne Place, Hove
East Sussex BN3 1HF, England

Printed in Italy
Phototypeset by Granada Graphics Limited